Friends of the Flowers

A Curious Tale of Priceless Pollinators

For Cassandra

written and illustrated by

Kenton R. Hill

Kenton R. Hill

LUMINARE PRESS
WWW.LUMINAREPRESS.COM

Friends of the Flowers
A Curious Tale of Priceless Pollinators
Written and illustrated by Kenton R. Hill © 2020

All rights reserved.
This book or any portion thereof may not be
reproduced or used in any manner whatsoever without
the express written permission of the publisher, except for the
use of brief quotations in a book review.

Printed in the United States of America

Cover and Interior Design by Claire Flint Last
Author Photo by Ed Keene

Luminare Press
442 Charnelton St.
Eugene, OR 97401

www.luminarepress.com

ISBN: 978-1-64388-466-0

> "The hum of bees is the voice of the garden."
> —Elizabeth Lawrence

To curious kids everywhere

No two flowers are alike
no two kids are alike
and each has
a unique contribution
to make in the world

Collect all FIVE books in the TALES OF CURIOUS CRITTERS series

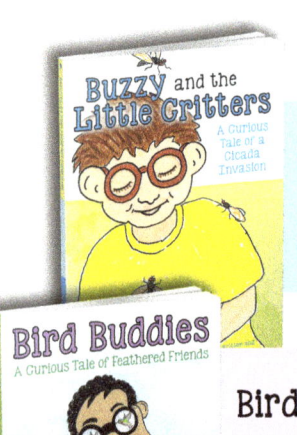

Buzzy and the Little Critters
A Curious Tale of a Cicada Invasion
(2016)

Bird Buddies
A Curious Tale of Feathered Friends
(2017)

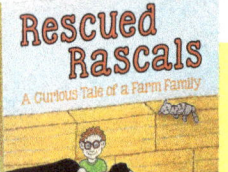

Rescued Rascals
A Curious Tale of a Farm Family
(2018)

Buddies on the Beach
A Curious Tale of Sharing the Sea with Sharks
(2019)

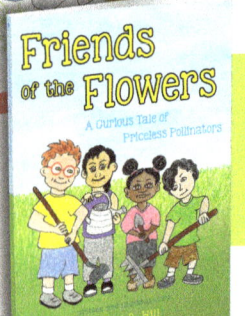

Friends of the Flowers
A Curious Tale of Priceless Pollinators
(2020)

Contents

1. The Sting 1
2. We Need Bees 3
3. Pollinator Pals 7
4. Bees, Butterflies, Beetles, and Birds 11
5. Preparing to Plant 15
6. Planting Plans 19
7. Being Bee Safe 23
8. Caring for the Gardens 27
9. The Midnight Shift 37
10. One More Bumble Bee Lesson 45

Glossary 49
Learning More 51
My Notes 52
Special Thanks 55
One More Fun Fact 56

Friends of the Flowers

-1-
The Sting

"Ouch!"

Gus could hear his friend Gina screaming from next door.

"That hurt!!" she shouted again. Louder.

"What happened?" Gus yelled as he raced over to Gina's back yard.

"That good-for-nothing bee stung me!" Gina answered.

"That's not true," Gus said.

"I should know if I've been stung or not," Gina replied rubbing her hand where the bee stung her.

"It hurts. It felt like a shot at the doctor's office. It's hot and itchy," Gina said, trying to hold back her tears.

"I meant the 'good-for-nothing' part isn't true. We need bees. But I'm sorry you got stung. I know that hurts." Gus was feeling sad for his friend.

"I got stung once and it really hurt for a while, but a cold cloth and some pain medicine helped," Gus recalled. "Let's find your mom."

-2-
We Need Bees

A few days later when Gina was feeling better, she came over to see Gus and asked him, "What did you mean when you said 'we need bees' and that 'they aren't good-for-nothing'?"

"First, how is your hand?" Gus had been worried about his friend.

"Better. Thanks. The pain and the red swollen spot are almost gone." She held up her hand to show him. Her usual smile was back, "But really, why do we need bees?"

Gus answered Gina's question. "If we don't have bees we would have to live without about 1/3 of the foods we eat. These plants depend on bees to pollinate them so they can make seeds to make more plants."

"Without bees many plants like grapes, cranberries, melons, almonds, and apples would be gone."

"How did you get so smart?" Gina said, not really meaning it.

"I am only a little smart about pollination, but our neighbor, Mr. Bloom, is really smart. He told me about why we need all kinds of pollinators. Come on, let's go see him!" Gus headed across the street with Gina right behind.

Mr. Bloom was working in his garden as usual. "Hi kids. What's up with you today?"

"Well, Gina got stung by a bee a few days ago," Gus began.

"Oh, I am sorry to hear that. Are you okay now?" Mr. Bloom asked.

Gina nodded 'yes' and then asked, "Do we really need bees?"

"You bet we do. Without bees we would have to live without about 1/3 of the foods we eat." Mr. Bloom's answer sounded just like what Gus had said.

Gus smiled. He was happy that Mr. Bloom agreed that bees were not good-for-nothings, but more like little heroes.

-3-
Pollinator Pals

Mr. Bloom loves to garden. He used to be a botanist—a scientist who studies plants. So, next to gardening his favorite thing is teaching people about plants—especially kids.

Mr. Bloom could see Gina and Gus were interested so he asked, "Do you know about pollination? It is the reason why bees and other critters are so important to plants."

Gina answered for both of them, "We sorta do, but you can tell us."

"Here is how it works. Bees visit flowers to collect food. They drink up nectar and gather a powder called pollen on their legs and bodies," Mr. Bloom began to explain.

"Pollen? Is that why they call it pollination?" Gus asked.

"Yes, and as bees fly from flower to flower they take the pollen from the male part of the flower, the stamen, and take it to the pistil, the female part of the flower—where it needs to be to become seeds."

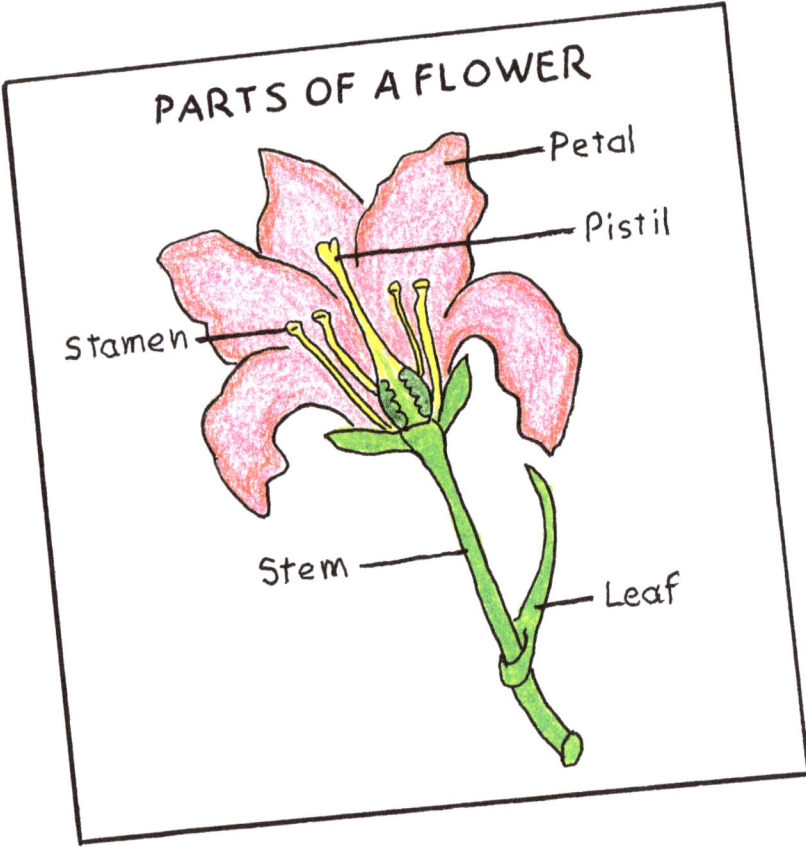

Mr. Bloom pointed out the flower parts as he explained. "Seeds are what make more plants, and make foods for us and for wildlife too."

"You said other critters are important to plants like bees. What did you mean?" Gina was eager to learn more.

"Bees have lots of pollinator pals. Flies, bats, other animals and even the wind can move pollen from one flower to another. But, the pollinators I encourage to come to my garden along with bees are butterflies, beetles, and birds—hummingbirds to be exact," Mr. Bloom continued.

"You know I could use some help with my garden. It is a big garden as you can see."

"And now that Mrs. Bloom is ill and can't work outside with me, I really could use some help. You could learn more about plants and pollination as we work together," Mr. Bloom said hopefully.

"We will have to ask our parents, but it sounds good to me. How does it sound to you, Gus?" Gina was ready to help.

"Thanks, Mr. Bloom. We will be back as soon as we talk to our parents!" Gus was as excited as Gina.

-4-
Bees, Butterflies, Beetles, and Birds

Gina and Gus were not alone when they ran back to Mr. Bloom and his garden. Gus's big brother, Boone, and their friend, Rosa were there too. All four were ready to help with the garden and to learn more.

"Okay. Here's how you can help. I can take care of the vegetables out back, but Mrs. Bloom would like you to take care of the flower garden and add more flowering plants." Mr. Bloom was so happy to have a team of junior gardeners reporting for duty.

Gina spoke up, "I have an idea. There are four of us and four corners in the garden. Maybe each one of us could have our own corner. One for each of your favorite pollinators."

Before Mr. Bloom could say, "That's a good idea!" Rosa, who has always been more than fond of hummingbirds, said, "I would love to take care of the bird corner!"

Mr. Bloom barely had time to go ahead and say, "That's a good idea!" when Boone, famous for his curiosity about insects, volunteered to take the beetle corner.

Gus followed quickly with, "Dibs on the butterfly corner."

That left Gina. She was not too happy that the only pollinators left were bees. Her hand had healed, but the memory of the sting had not left her.

Mr. Bloom could see Gina was not sure she wanted to take the bee corner so he offered, "There are things you can do to stay safe around bees. I can teach you if you would like me to."

With that Gina took a deep breath and said, "Okay. I can do it. Let's get started."

-5-
Preparing to Plant

"Before we plant we need a plan," Mr. Bloom announced. "Each of you has picked your pollinator. Next you will need to figure out what plants will attract them.

"I have some books you can borrow, but I am sure you will come up with other ideas on your own."

"Mrs. Hoffman at the library always has good suggestions. We can ask her for help finding the right books," Boone suggested.

"And I can go online to see what we can find out," Rosa said —always ready to check out the latest on her laptop.

"I can ask my teacher, Mr. Carver. He knows a lot about science," Gina was sure he could help.

"My grandma has one of the best flower gardens I have ever seen. I'll bet she knows what butterflies like." Gus was really ready to get going.

Mr. Bloom was impressed, "Those are all great ideas! When you have your plans in mind come see me and we will get to work planting together.

"While you do your plans I will get the soil ready. I have a great compost pile out back in my vegetable garden. I will mix it all into the ground."

"What's a compost pile?" Gus asked.

"What's in it?" Boone wondered.

And Gina also asked, "How does this compost thing work?"

Always ready to teach a lesson, Mr. Bloom answered, "The compost pile is made up of old grass clippings, leaves, vegetable peelings, fruit waste, plant clippings. Things like that.

"When you work that into the ground it's like food for the dirt. A natural fertilizer. Plants and flowers grow better when you put compost into the soil."

With that, Mr. Bloom began to prepare the soil, and the four young gardeners ran off to figure out what flowers they needed to attract their pollinator pals.

All four of the eager young gardeners were quick to do their research and get back to Mr. Bloom with their lists of flowers that they wanted him to buy for their corner of the garden.

Gus was first to arrive with his list.

-6-
Planting Plans

Dear Mr. Bloom,
I want to attract monarch butterflies. To start I will need these flowers:

- Milkweed—where lady monarchs can lay their eggs and caterpillars can eat the leaves.
- Also some butterfly weed.
- Then for early spring some:
- Zinnia
- Cosmos
- For late summer:
- Goldenrods
- Meadow blazing star

And my Grandma said all flowers should be "native". That means they should belong in the area where we live.

Thank you,
GUS

Rosa was right behind Gus with her list.

Hello Mr. Bloom,

There is a long list of flowers that hummingbirds like so any of these should bring them to our fun new garden.

- ~ Columbine
- ~ Coral honeysuckle
- ~ Salvia
- ~ Coleus
- ~ Fuchsia

Hummingbirds also love to take baths. A fountain and bird bath would be great.

Thank you,
ROSA

Next to deliver his list of flowers to buy was Boone.

Yo Mr. B.

I think it would be fun to see if we could attract some flower longhorn beetles.

They are pretty good pollinators. They like flat open flower blossoms like asters, hydrangeas, magnolias, night-blooming phlox, and I think they also like roses— wild roses.

But, I learned that bugs called aphids like roses too. And aphids are not good for roses.

So, if we plant some wild roses we should get some ladybugs because they like to eat aphids.

Thanks,
BOONE

And finally Gina delivered her wish list of flowers to Mr. Bloom.

Hello Mr. Bloom,

I think bumble bees will be really good for all kinds of berries-peppers and tomatoes too.

The flowers I learned bumble bees like early in the spring are:

~ Lilac, Heather, and Bee Balm

And later they like:

~ Sunflowers, Dahlias, and Evening Primroses.

But, remember you were going to tell me more about how to be safe around bees. Maybe we should do that before we plant a garden to attract more stingers.

Thank you,
GINA

-7-
Being Bee Safe

"Gina, you wanted me to talk about how to be safe around bees, right?" Mr. Bloom asked.

Gina was ready. "Yes. What should I know?"

"First of all, bumble bees are large, but they are quite gentle. When they are collecting nectar they are so busy and focused you can easily pet their fuzzy little bodies.

"However, I wouldn't recommend that. But, they are often called the friendly bee," Mr. Bloom began.

"That sting on my hand didn't seem friendly to me," Gina recalled.

"Like most wild bees they are not aggressive and don't sting unless they are threatened or think you are attacking them.

"Did you swat at the bee or try to slap the bee that stung you?" Mr. Bloom wondered.

"I did and I tried to run away, but it caught up with me and stung me," Gina remembered clearly.

"Well, here are some things you can do to encourage bees to leave you alone." Mr. Bloom, the botanist, was ready to deliver another lesson.

"To begin, you can create a place for them to live safely. You can let them nest in your yard—in woodpiles, compost heaps, rockeries or in the ground.

"And you can be sure you plant the flowers that keep them happy and healthy.

"But you don't want to look like a flower or smell like a flower yourself.

"Bees can smell strong scents and can confuse perfumes and colognes for nectar of flowers. And some people think if you are wearing brightly colored clothes that can attract them too. I am not so sure of that."

"Is that why beekeepers wear white outfits when they work with a honey bee hive?" Gina asked.

"Exactly. They also wear tight fitting clothes with tight cuffs on their sleeves and pant legs so bees can't get in. And thinking further about what to wear, I would remind you not to go barefoot if you have clover blossoms or small flowers in your lawn. If you step on or near a bee it is not going to like that.

"Being careful of what you eat when you are near bees is also a good idea. Sugary drinks and foods like fruits can attract bees and definitely attract wasps. So, be sure not to leave apple cores or orange peels lying around."

Mr. Bloom finished his lesson with one final piece of advice. "And remember, you can blow on a bee if it lands on you. That usually makes it go away. But the worst thing you can do is to swat at it or make it feel trapped. Just stay still. Stay calm. Take a deep breath or two while the bee checks you out. When the bee sees you are not a flower and are of no use to it, the bee will fly away."

Gina laughed and wondered, "Did you just say a bee would call me a 'good-for-nothing' human being?"

-8-
Caring for the Gardens

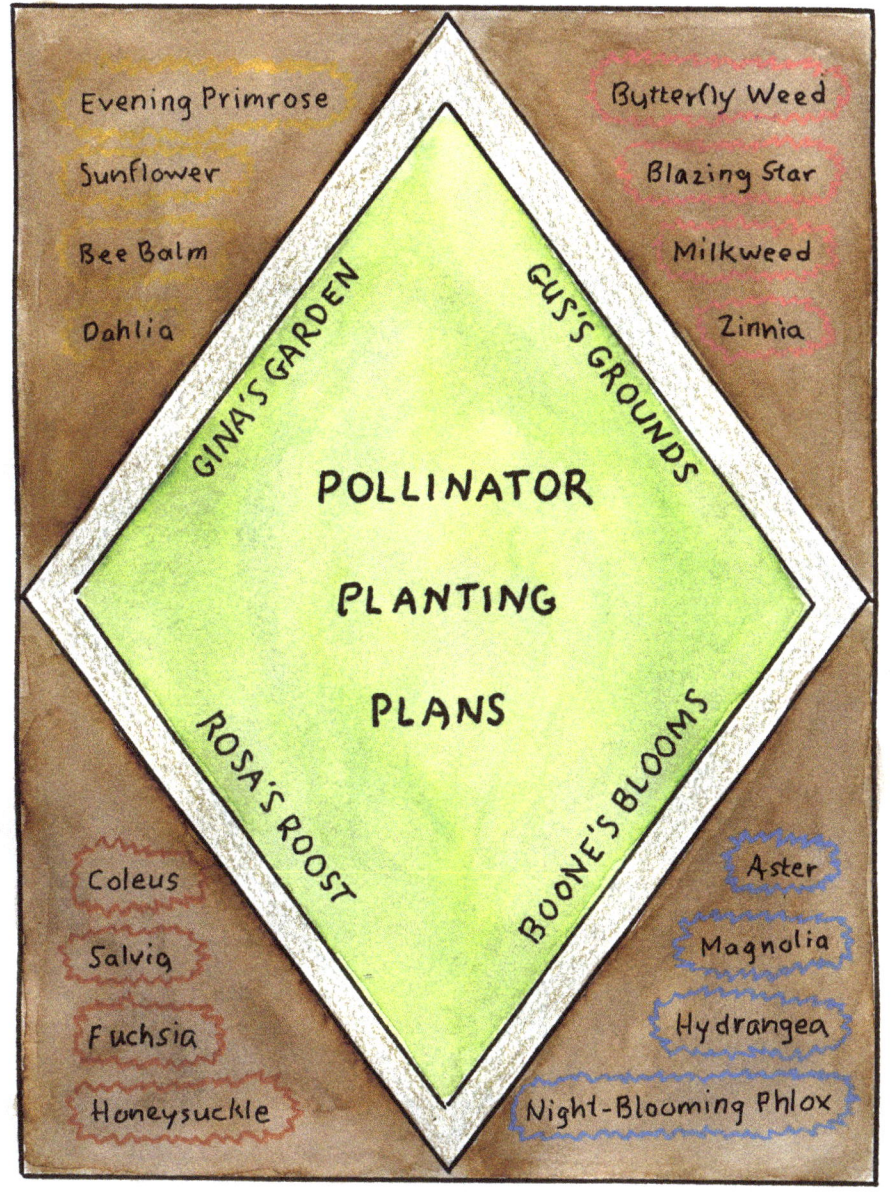

"I learned that it helps butterflies if you plant lots of the same color flowers in large clumps. That way they can spot them when flying over the garden.

"It's also a good idea to plant clumps of different kinds of flowers that bloom at different times of the year. And you have to start with milkweed."

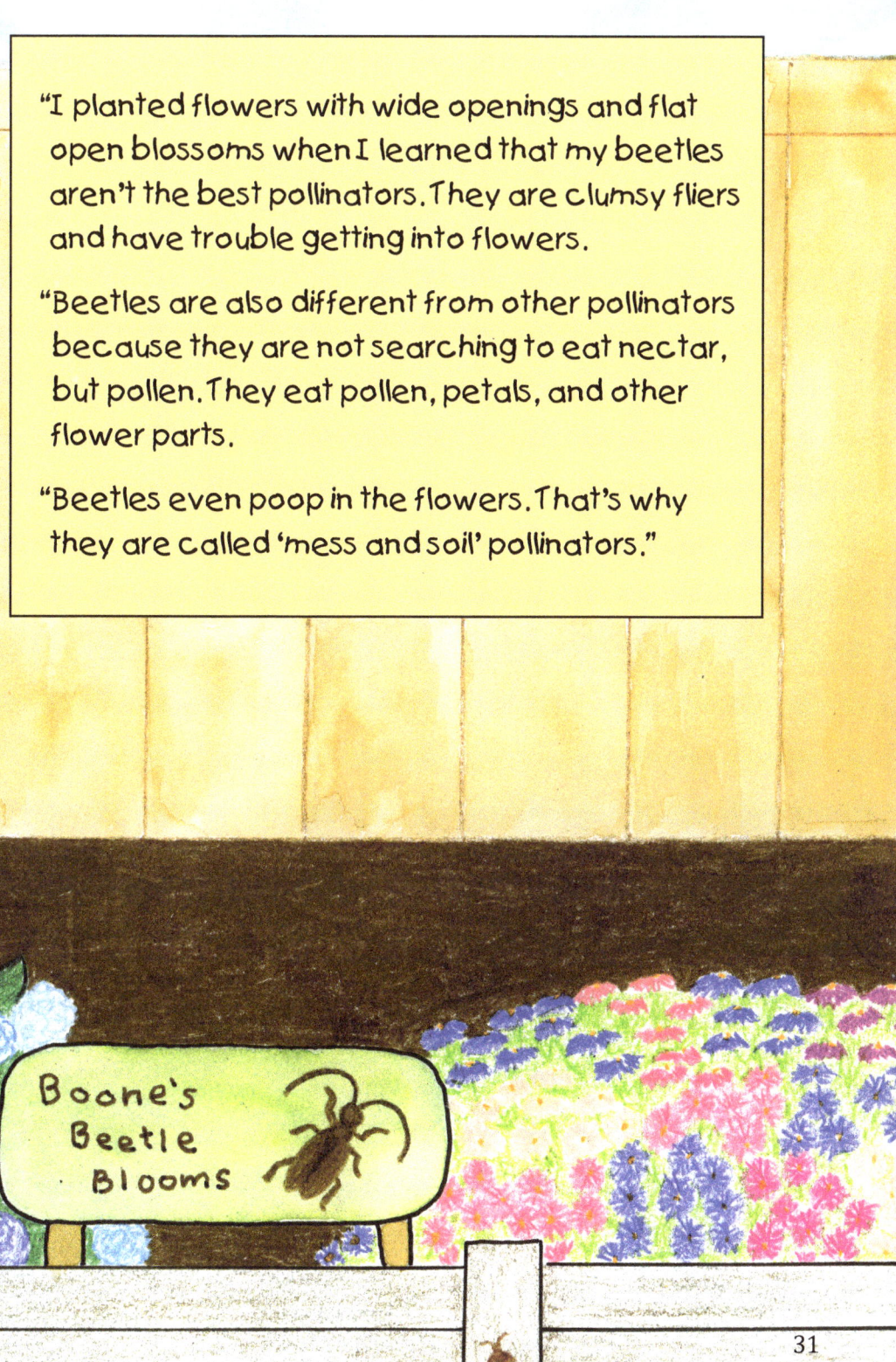

"I planted flowers with wide openings and flat open blossoms when I learned that my beetles aren't the best pollinators. They are clumsy fliers and have trouble getting into flowers.

"Beetles are also different from other pollinators because they are not searching to eat nectar, but pollen. They eat pollen, petals, and other flower parts.

"Beetles even poop in the flowers. That's why they are called 'mess and soil' pollinators."

"My hummingbirds love my garden with its bird bath fountain. They also love all of the flowers that are shaped like their long beaks. It makes it easier for them to get to the nectar inside of the flowers. And the pollen can land on their foreheads so they can take it to the next flower.

"I have to tell my 'bee friend' Gina I learned that there is a hummingbird called the bee hummingbird. It's called that because it is only two inches long and is 'as busy as a bee' pollinating up to 1,500 flowers a day."

"I've learned a lot since that bee stung me. For one thing, I learned that I can thank a bee or some other pollinator for one in every three bites of food I take. And like most critters, the bees won't hurt you if you don't bother them while they are doing their job. So, no more stings for me!

"Besides the flowers I have planted to attract bees, Mr. Bloom has also planted what they call a 'bee lawn'. It is a mix of lawn grass and low-growing flowers that bloom again after mowing.

"That means I can't go barefoot in the lawn, but that's okay because it means we have a lot more of those 'good-for-something' bees."

Weeks went by as Rosa, Gus, Gina and Boone watered, weeded, and admired their flower gardens. They were all very proud that they had made their dreams of attracting pollinators come true.

-9-
The Midnight Shift

But, there was one question that had been bugging Gus. "Every day we see our beetles, bees, birds, and butterflies flying in and out and all around our gardens doing their job of pollinating. But, did you ever wonder who does the work at night?"

Rosa jumped in ready to brag, "I'm sure it is my hummingbirds. They are the hardest workers of them all."

"And just how do they see at night?" asked Gus.

"It's like radar. They make their high-pitched humming sound. It bounces off the petals of the flowers so they can tell where the flowers are, and that lets them pollinate all night long." Rosa answered as if she really believed it was true.

"No way!" Boone interrupted. "It's my flower longhorn beetles who do the pollinating work at night. They learned how to read the garden even blinded by the dark. It's like braille—using their antenna to feel their way from flower to flower."

Gina shook her head and said, "No. My bees are the ones. No radar. No braille. Lightning bugs. That's how they do it. Each bee has a lightning bug buddy who shines the way, makes it easy to see the flowers and to pollinate throughout the night."

"Those are all cute stories, but if you want to know who really does the pollination at night it is my butterflies," Gus was ready to try to make them believe his story of how it really happens.

"And just how do your butterflies see at night?" They all wanted to know.

"Easy. Night vision goggles. They can see the whole garden all night long." That was Gus's answer.

Everybody liked their own idea best, but they all headed home still curious about what really happens in their gardens at night.

Boone was the most curious. That night he couldn't get to sleep. He kept thinking about night pollinators. He got up several times—looking out his bedroom window across the street at the Bloom's house. Wondering…

"I can't stand it any longer," Boone said quietly to himself. He didn't want to wake up his brother, Gus. He grabbed his phone to use as a flashlight, and still in his PJs he tiptoed out the door and headed to the flower garden.

Boone began to search the flowers with his phone flashlight, looking for any sign of midnight pollinators. He was having no luck.

"Maybe there are no night-time pollinators," he said sadly to himself. "But what about my night-blooming phlox and the evening primrose that Gina planted? Who pollinates them?"

Boone kept looking until he was startled by a rustling sound behind him. He cautiously turned around. And there was Gus! His brother had heard Boone leave and he had followed him to the garden.

"You scared me! What are you doing here?" Boone asked.

"Same as you. Looking for pollinators in the night. And I think I found something. Bring your flashlight over here," Gus whispered excitedly.

Sure enough there in the night were three moths fluttering among the yellow primrose plants. Three hawk moths doing their job.

Luckily, Boone had his phone with him. He snapped a picture, "Now we can show Rosa and Gina that there were no superheroes, no radar, no lightning bugs, no braille, no night vision goggles," Boone began.

And Gus finished, "Just one more little critter to add to our list of pollinators: Bees, butterflies, beetles, birds, and now the midnight moths!"

That ends our *Curious Tale of Priceless Pollinators.*

But not really…

—Because the kids kept weeding and watering their gardens.

—The flowers kept blooming.

—The pollinators kept pollinating.

—The kids kept learning.

—Mrs. Bloom kept smiling as she admired the flowers from her window. And she said to the four young gardeners, "Each of you is like a beautiful flower. And together you have become a gorgeous bouquet."

—Mr. Bloom kept feeding the soil and being sure that any insecticides used to protect the plants were safe.

And of course…

—Mr. Bloom kept teaching. He especially thought the more Gina knew about bumble bees the more she would appreciate them and the less likely she would be to ever be afraid again.

-10-
One More Bumble Bee Lesson From Mr. Bloom

1. There are at least 20,000 different kinds of bees in the world.

2. Bees come in all shapes and sizes, from metallic green bees the size of your pinky fingernail to fuzzy black and yellow bumble bees.

3. There are about 50 kinds of bumble bees in North America and 250 kinds in the world.

4. Bumble bees are among the first bees to be seen in the spring and the last bees out in the fall. You can help support bumble bees by planting flowers that will bloom between April and October.

5. Bumble bees like to nest in protected spaces that look messy, such as rock piles, near the base of a thick shrub, or even in an old mouse burrow.

6. At the largest size during the summer, a bumble bee colony (group) can have anywhere from 50 to 1,000 worker (female) bees buzzing around.

7. Many colonies don't make it through the summer because of badgers, disease, being poisoned by pesticides, not enough flowers or climate change.

8. The bumble bees that do make it through the summer have an annual cycle, meaning the colony only lives for one year. This is how it works:

SPRING: The queen bee has been hibernating all winter long underground, and is woken up by the warming temperature. She finds a good place to nest, collects food from early spring flowers and then begins to lay eggs. In 4 to 5 weeks the eggs will become adult female worker bees.

SUMMER: The queen bee has produced many worker bees by this time, and no longer has to leave the nest for food. While the queen stays home to lay eggs, worker bees buzz around cleaning and protecting the colony, and collecting lots of pollen and nectar to feed the entire colony. Just before fall season, new queens will be produced and mate with male bumble bees (drones).

FALL: After making new queens, the old queen, worker bees, and male bees will die off. The new queen visits the last couple of blooming flowers to stock up on food, and will search for a nice place to hibernate.

WINTER: The queen sleeps all winter long in a safe cavity she built beneath leaves, pine needles, or maybe a thick layer of grass.

9. That is what I can tell you now.

But, we scientists still have a lot to learn about bees and all the other curious critters.

Glossary

1. Antenna—feelers on head of an insect
2. Aphid—small insect that sucks sap from plants
3. Beekeeper—person who raises honey bees
4. Botanist—scientist who studies plants
5. Braille—for people who have difficulty seeing—a special form of writing with raised dots in patterns that represent letters
6. Chemicals—man-made products to use in the garden
7. Cologne—sweet smelling liquid
8. Compost—mix of old leaves and manure used to improve the soil
9. Fertilizer—chemical or natural material put on or in the soil to help plants grow
10. Larvae—newly hatched, wingless insect
11. Life-cycle—the different stages a creature goes through in a lifetime

12. Native Plants—plants that grow on their own in a given part of the country and provide food and shelter for pollinators and other wildlife

13. Nectar—sweet liquid in flowers eaten by insects and hummingbirds

14. Night Vision Goggles—glasses used to see in the dark

15. Perfume—substance that gives off the smell of a flower

16. Pistil—the female part of a flower

17. Pollen—the fine powder-like grains produced inside of seed plants

18. Pollination—the carrying of pollen from one flower's male part (stamen) to another flower's female part (pistil)

19. Pupae—an insect between the time of hatching (larva) and becoming an adult

20. Radar—a way of finding objects by bouncing sound off of them

21. Stamen—the male part of a flower

22. Sting—something Gina never wants to happen ever again!

Learning More

If you want to learn more about flowers and pollinators here are some ideas:

Visit your local library

Tell the librarian what you are looking for—they love to help!

Read other books like:

Attracting Birds, Butterflies, and Other Backyard Wildlife
By David Mizejewski

Give Bees a Chance
By Bethany Barton

Incredible Insects (coloring book)
By Christopher Marley

Mini Meadows:
Grow a Little Patch of Colorful Flowers Anywhere around Your Yard
By Mike Lizotte

The Little Book of Bees
By Hilary Kearney

Wake Up, Woods
By Michael Homoya

MY NOTES

MY NOTES

"Everything stinks until it is finished"

—DR. SEUSS

Special Thanks

To those who helped me "finish" my story

Lucile Burt
Poet/Teacher
Wellfleet, Massachusetts

Jana Hoffman
Supervising Librarian
Leeding Library
Milwaukie, Oregon

Katie Lamke
Bumble Bee Conservation Specialist
The Xerces Society
Lincoln, Nebraska

Stephanie McKale
Retired 3rd and 4th Grade Teacher
East School
New Canaan, Connecticut

Dr. Lauren Ponisio
Associate Professor
Department of Biology
University of Oregon
Eugene, Oregon

Leslie Rennie-Hill
Wife and Sharer of Many Good Ideas
Portland, Oregon

One More Fun Fact

Dr. Roscoe E. Hill, Ken's father, was a professor of entomology (a scientist who studies insects) at the University of Nebraska from 1946 until 1976. He served as the Chairman of the Department of Entomology from 1950 to 1966.

While he was doing his research on bees for his Master's Degree in 1936 he discovered a new strand of bees.

The new bee was named
Coelioxys bisoncornua Hill, 1936

CPSIA information can be obtained
at www.ICGtesting.com
Printed in the USA
BVHW020305050222
628035BV00004B/58